TO CHASE THE SUN

CRAIG RANDALL

Copyright © 2022 by Craig Randall

All rights reserved.

ISBN: 979-8-9856627-3-3

Cover Art by: @coverdungeondragon

Distributed by: Amazon KDP and Ingram Spark

Published by: Switchboard Publishing

No part of this book may be reproduced in any form or by any electronic or mechanical means, including information storage and retrieval systems, without written permission from the author, except for the use of brief quotations in a book review.

Also by Craig Randall

The Doom that Came to Astoria: The Northwest Trilogy Part 1

DEDICATIONS

This book is dedicated first and foremost to my wife and children. For their grace and love and for their adventurous hearts.

Next, to my friends and family. For the wonderful years of encouragement and support.

Also, to Anna Druse and Andy West. The best two English Lit. teachers ever! Thank you for unlocking a passion I didn't even know was there.

Lastly, to my students who have inspired me each and every day and filled me with hope.

"Make not your thoughts
your prisons."

William Shakespeare

INTRODUCTION

If a person lives in darkness long enough, their vision can blur. We can *learn wrong* to mistake it for the light—thinking that's all there is. Or at least grow far too comfortable thinking you don't deserve the light.

Like many people, I've struggled with anxiety and depression my whole life. It was a dark cloud that hung over my every moment, but like many of us, I got really, really great at faking it. Which only makes everything worse. For years, I struggled in the same silent way so many do. Constant fear, relentless wave after wave of negative self-talk crashing down, one after another, always keeping me un-rooted in who I actually was. Perpetual terror that everything, at every moment, would collapse all at once and consume me.

Then, a breakthrough came. Through a series of powerful experiences, I could at last admit to myself the truth of my depressive state.

The interesting thing, looking back, is how a combination of pride and misconceptions of strength and masculinity kept me from seeking help, a healthier lifestyle, and hope.

I went to therapy—which was brilliant! But told no one.

INTRODUCTION

Through our discussions, I learned how severe the problem was, but also learned there was hope. Restoration was possible. I learned there was something in me worth saving. Thus began my journey towards healing.

Growth is not a linear process, and I spent the next several years with significant trials, on and off medication, as I wrestled with what I thought being "okay" should look like. One night, I was exercising to take my mind off the spinning panic and I spun out. Hard! I collapsed, fell back, back against the wall and lost it.

I'd read earlier that afternoon that some people find solace in writing a play-by-play of what they're feeling when they're in a spin. I grabbed my phone and let the words fly.

Twenty minutes later, calm returned. It sort of worked, but I left it at that and returned to life.

A few days later, it happened again, and again I grabbed my phone and wrote.

This time, though, I actually re-read what I'd written and, to my shock, found quite a rhythm to it. Poetry. Very dark and dismal, but poetic.

It happened several more times over the next few weeks, but I'd started writing.

After, I'd been reading a brilliant book on the plasticity of the brain and how we can train it to think in new ways. It highlighted the research that says what we focus on and speak and think and say will guide the long-term, more subconscious patterns we build. This terrified me a bit. How many years had I let negative thinking drive me?

I had an idea.

Returning to my depressing poems, I added what I'd been teaching my students about in our poetry unit. Voltas and shifts. How a poem can change from one thing to another in a way a writer might infer toward meaning.

INTRODUCTION

Then I had several poems that started from my rooted anxious thoughts but turned, by the end, towards hope.

It felt...*good*.

The next time the spin came, I grabbed my phone and started writing. It was different this time, though. I wrote the shift right into it and something magical happened.

The feelings? All the spinning negativity? It went away. It faded like mist after the sun had burned itself through a cover of cloud.

It might have been one of the single most exciting and naturally intoxicating moments of my life.

It changed everything and led to an explosion of creativity, the start of which is what you're holding in your hands right now.

I started practicing. Writing with different shapes and structures. I adopted the haiku for practical purposes. They're short and you can insert a little turn/shift/volt right in the middle or the last line, and in a short amount of time, create a quick but powerful shift in your own mind!

To Chase the Sun was born.

I published these poems in the order their written order, in the different states of mind I found myself in throughout the healing process: Chaos, Order, and Beyond. They represent my concrete search for hope and how my entire world changed once I found it.

The chaos section of this collection represents the almost word-vomit as it engaged concretely with the feelings and the negativity. They are the poems that reconciled me to the fact that these problems existed. That I wasn't well and wished to be. To me, they represent one side of the spectrum of healing. My mind, all over the place, desperately wanting to be well, but without the ability to take form or shape. I feel myself, in these poems, recognizing the change I wanted to make, but I wasn't sure how yet.

INTRODUCTION

My journey led me towards certain exercises where I could use words to shape my thoughts, to take back control, and to make order out of the chaos. Hence the next stage: Order.

As if often the human experience, we tend to rubber band from one thing to another, a few times even, before things feel steady and even out.

That's where these poems came from.

Something about anxiety that many rarely understand (if you've never suffered from it chronically), is that rules get created. Rules that if we just live by them...then we think everything will be okay. It staves off certain feelings for a while, but it's still not healthy. After too long, it becomes a prison.

There was a time, midway through writing the poems, which grew into this collection, when form followed function. I leaned into pre-prescribed poetic forms to place my generated thoughts. At the advice of a therapist and books I'd read on the brain and neuroplasticity, I began weaving a series of consistent thoughts into my mind and placing them metaphorically into these poetic frames.

It changed everything.

Within a few weeks, my moods lightened. My heart and mind and thoughts lifted, for longer periods of time, at least. My wife, family and friends saw noticeable changes in me.

Order existed. And safety. My mind had become a place I could let my guard down again, and I'd carved out a new access point to the more positive and optimistic pathway in my mind. But it felt stronger and deeper.

Over time, yes, I showed improvement; moved forward, yet I rubber-banded to the other side of the spectrum. Rigidity. Rules. Hyper-structure. To a chronically anxious person, this structure equates to security, but when it tips, it crumbles. Quick. Unfortunately, it becomes a cage of its own.

INTRODUCTION

The answer came as a balanced ebb and flow of the two, learning to navigate the tension of having wings and a solid root system. After rubber-banding back and forth between extremes, I started learning how to use authentic words and the scaffolding as the foundation for moving beyond.

Certain things clicked. I felt it in my mind, my being, my writing, my life. Everything. And everywhere.

I didn't mean the struggle was gone or that shadows never crept. It meant, to me, that the more optimistic pathway had been dug, giving me the chance, moment by moment, to choose hope and light and life.

My hope—my end goal beyond using writing as a means to heal—is that this book can represent the possibilities that exist in each of us, of restoration, of healing, and of hope.

I lived so much of my life in the darkness, I'd learned to believe it was all there was. Pain became an unfortunate comfort, only by consistency and association, but not by choice. If we choose, we can move out of whatever feelings we have, and/or circumstance, and we have the power to build whatever life we want. I believe that.

Where are you at right now? Still in the darkness? In the pain? Or have you stumbled onto the path to healing?

Just know how brilliant and powerful you are. Know what you're capable of, and your choices will guide your steps to what you want.

The world needs each of us to be the fullest versions of ourselves we can. It needs us to love and create and build to not just make ourselves whole, but our families and homes and communities along with us.

PREFACE

Imagine

Imagine --
Imagine catching a tornado
Pin-balling
Back and forth
Off
The inside of your skull,

With only a butterfly net...

Now --
Now, imagine all you need, truly, is
To reach out into the stillness, grasp, and hold
Tight, hold tight to peace, The Confidence of True:

To know --
To know that if you leave the net behind,
Reach out with your hand,
And are still,
The butterfly will come to you.

Imagine

Imagine—
Imagine the come-around,
  in nature,
that made us.
    Or
  The inside: carbohydrate.

With only a boring mutation.

Now—
Now imagine all you need, only is,
To reach out into the illness, grasp, and build
a tight, holding tighter pattern. The Continent goes blue.

to know—
To know that, even to see the net behind,
gives an work your hand.
    And are still.
    The bottle keys it down to your.

CHAOS

Fractured: a study of self

Am I me, of right now, or
Am I me of then, or all the iterations
Of before that led to now?

Broken and healed only
To break once more -
Free, yet caged, ebbing back
Between those chains forged both by
That self and other
Selves, not of *my* own doing.

Am I the self un-medicated, lost
To emotion's swirls, those slate whims, those
Eroding thoughts? Or
Am I the medicated torrent, stilled and
Controlled - the dam
Has burst, yet - somehow - I hold myself
At bay.

Which and *Who* am I? The person I
Objectively feel I am
To be

The current self, I know now, is unsure.

I tempt posterity to believe
How others see *my* self - and why.

Water falling
Raging or a still, small
Running stream, following preset

Bounds onward through
Concurrent shores.

I am reassured by those others, whose
Presence brings enough assurance, that I am of
The latter thoughts.

As to the former, I assume, the living thoughts for
Those I have not the bravery to ask.

Am I, are We, not simply several complex selves, of
Times and places where we have occupied in
Previous states?

Am I bound by the self or am I truly
Free to become what *new* choice dictates?

Is the cage merely built by
Me, myself alone?

To what responsibility are *others*?

Constraints - such founded on assumptions, built thereof
By grueling mental toil and laid, brick by brick, to ensnare.
Built by *these* hands, knowing *now* that can, with *these* hand's
Intention, be taken down. Thrown off. Cast afar.
Dismantled and left discarded -

To fade as I imbue myself with vibrant hues

Is this the real which I seek? My many selves?

Is the truth that I am who I aim or choose to be? Therefore

Those other selves have no voice, save what power *they* receive
From *me?*

Let it burn, then, and amidst what ash and residue remains, I Will
Build a sturdy self that *will* endure the flame, the self inflicted Torment

And unlock the door
And take apart the cage
From within.

Free to burn. Free to, simply, *be*

Beauty

Sometimes I wonder
if when sadness leaves its mark upon
those certain souls we see,
it is not they who are broken, who
are cracked, like
remnant clay of distant times -
but the world Itself.

It's indifference and jealousy
gives way to hidden truth,
lost in misunderstanding,
Whether with intention or of lack,
does not justify such pain.

For the world itself is *taken* by the
beatific resonant stirrings from these elevated
brave.

It is *It*, not they, who has caused this
separation - stemming the belonging
sought so rightly by those whose hearts are
in need of home.

It was *It*, not they, not *you*, friend, who
caused the grave partition.

May *It's* hold on you fall and fade, and

may your beauty Shine. May it Rage and then Uproot. May
the fierceness in you rise,
for *you* are one worthy of worlds to be built -- to replace the
slow and cold

orbit that *It* made around a sun - let it set one final time,
for a fresh world to dawn anew --
To blossom and unfold --
And sing --
To sing --
Of you.

Then and Now

      Between
     Then and Now,
          I am.

    Cliched feet
harbor jealousy for
  what will
        Become.

Backward glances
     ring
      of
    Peace:
still and faded,
    forgotten
    photos
  future Hopes
   and Dreams
     lingering
on the very edge
  of the space
    within our
      minds.

Two worlds with
edges sharp, as
newly printed
    paper.

    Warm to my
      finger's
          touch.

     This gives
       life -

     This lifts
       soul -

    This will not
      can not
        change
what lies
        behind
    beneath
    but,

This that started
  then, can and
    will
   lead you
    onto
    now.

Twirl

To spin and twirl out
-side my natural meter,
is to fly, my feet still
dragging, firm, upon the
ground. To wish to
leave the stratosphere,
and higher go than any
plane, I know, would be a
dream of comfort gone
- there twirls and spins
are welcome. In time, my
spirit stretched and grown,
to know and understand
that days might come - will
come, I know, where feet
will leap and leave behind
those silly limitations, those
prison bars in-placed by
others, yet, held by me - my
mind - the walls of wrecking.
Our thoughts, mine own, the
tipping point, to hold the spin,
increase the speed, it is not
control, as much, release,
from holding tight, to twirl,
weightless
and
free
...

Dust and Stone

I found a stone
the other
day,
and pick'd it up -
it caught my
eye.
It's beauty made me
wonder of it's
story,

it's start.

Those grains of sand,
compressed in
time
by pressure.
Years
And years - was it
anguish? Was it
painful?

Does it vary by
where it's
from?

Forrest floors
Or deserts dry.
Oceans vast or
rivers running by?

The conditions must be

ample in progressive
formulation of
each and
anything
with form.

No stones are
twins, nor are
they alike, save
for their carbon
base. Some smooth with
wash and wear. Some
jagged, scorched by
searing sun - cry out for
wholeness - striving to be
complete. Over
time, enough
grains
will
separate, and with
hope they will
return to where
it all
 began.

Back to dust and
once more
made.

The Mind pt. 1

shattered
shards grace
the floor
beneath the
mirror

two variant
selves, still
at odds

Pruning

peel back these petals
cracked, and shed them from
my mind

Rise

I was born to live
   - to feel and fall -
 - to stumble -
    and then,
whether with
great struggle
    -and-
     -or-
   with
  simple ease,
- a false but eager
  step - poised yet
  at times
    unpositioned -
For this
    was I -
were we -
   born
    to rise

Whole

    The heart
        The brain
    The mind
        The soul,
    Are,
    Some times,
At   ...   odds.

    The
      More
  Lined
    Up they
  Can become
- finding a focal
  center or
  connective
    point -
    The
    More
    At
    Peace
    I
    Become.

Paint By Numbers

I used to think
that life
was
Paint by Numbers

At least
that's what I
was
told and what
too
did tell

now

I just want to
throw some paint around
the room,
follows whims
and nudges
as they lead,
and see what
happens

What could
be the harm?

The Lie

It is a mountain
I am learning
to call out
and down.

To command -
so *it* will
listen - so it's
Strength
will
*b*end
and,
in time,
*b*reak
at My voice.

Now,
I call out, loud,
and bring
it to it's
*k*nees

Orbit

lost in space, I forgot what I was orbiting

ORDER

Yearn

Just as:
I long, in times
of rain, for
sunlight to
break through -

And so:
I yearn, in times
of pain, for
deep joy and
rest to sooth.

Thunderous

thunderous are the
searing lies, told crooked by
my traitorous mind

Look Not for Darkness

look not for darkness
in the world, change will come when
purged from my own heart

Silhouettes

dawn burns away the
silhouettes that haunt the night,
revealing true form

Smoke from Fire

thoughts can lift like smoke
from fire, be careful which you
choose - and how - to burn

Let the Oceans Sing

we must learn to let
the oceans sing their peace, to
rage until they sleep

Yellow Leaves

yellow leaves fall as
time churns ever on, but lo, for
green, once more, will grow

Raindrops

raindrops drip from leaves
above, and fall to little
pools below, to rest

Rushing Streams

stars reflect off water
clear and calm, bid me pause to
halt the rushing streams

Beware the Ice and Melting Snows

beware the ice and
melting snows, when springtime comes,
rivers will run high

The Nighttime Sky

the nighttime sky,
porch light of the heavens, a
guiding map to home

Let New Days Begin

let new days begin,
burn and bloom, potential hope
and resurrection

Sometimes Healing

sometimes healing is
as close or far away as
letting go your grip

BEYOND

To Chase the Sun

to chase the sun's light
is to hope, but it's truest
roots were born in rain

Morning Light

Even when
  the larks
   refuse to sing,

My *being*
  still longs
  for morning,

When fires
   set the
    skies ablaze,

And hope
  begins it's
  forming.

Ocean Water Cool and Crisp

ocean water cool
and crisp, folding waves lap the
shores to find their rest

Winter Whispers

winter whispers to
me, restful reminders of
healing and warmth

Winter's Foliage and Fruit Will Fade

winter's foliage
and fruit will fade, but it's roots
shall run deep and strong

Spring Came on Slow This Year

spring came on slow
this year, but bade it's turn with
wisdom and patience

I Take My Thoughts with Me

I take the flashlight as I go,
Out through the fog that hugs me dear,
Before the children wake from sleep -
Before the forest creatures stir.

I take with me my jacket thick,
My scarf wrapped tightly round to warm,
Beyond the frosted firs so tall -
Beyond the frozen creek and bridge

I take my winter gloves and hat,
And travel past the hidden falls,
Above the sheer stone path I walk -
Above the vast farm-tread fields.

I take my wild thoughts with me,
Far deep into the wilderness,
To realign them, sort the soul -
To refashion my mind anew.

I bring my *self* when I return,
Prepared for what such needs arise,
Ready to build the peace they need -
Ready to lift and love and lead.

August's Burn

August's burn lay its mark upon our skin,
By night our spirits spark as life begins.
To think, that morning met we waterside,
As stars aligned, such love did we abide.

No knowledge of the other 'e day before.
No comprehension of the road in store.
Beauty did scorch its scent amidst the mind,
Such lofty summer smells to us remind.

Pure joy, in retrospect, now hand in hand,
Sun dried, firm soil do our feet now stand.
Years tumble down as time pulls future near,
While closer to my heart I hold you dear.

The fire tow'rs and tow'rs to bid me yearn
Seasons 'membrance of faithful August's burn.

Your Eyes are Islands

your eyes are islands,
of tropical ocean blue,
calm, rhythmic, and true

The Sweetness of Your Soul I see

the sweetness of your
soul I see, from lives we've built,
'twined by years, as one

Calla Lilies

calla lilies,
forever reminding me
of you

My Children

I see in them, all
I hold, in right, in wrong, what
change need be in me

May the Rainfall Be

may the rainfall be
not but the nourishment for
all my hopes to come

Good Day, Good Night

good morning to the
day ahead, so filled with toils,
and beauty too
-
good night fair day, now
rest your mind, for tomorrow
beckons tasks anew

At Sea's Edge

at sea's edge,
the patient moon awaits
its rightful turn

Crack the Shutters

crack the shutters, in
with the warmth of light, the cool
and crisp mountain air

The Stars, They Sing

the stars, they sing to
me of wonder, and fill me
with hunger for the new

Behold, The Lily

behold the lily,
stands tall and proud, resting
'on beauty and grace

Heralds of the Dawn

each raindrop disrupts
the early morning quiet
heralding the day

Crackling Fire

crackling fire and
high-backed chair, my restful mind
lost from page to page

I Find Peace of Heart

as autumn makes its
subtle turns with trees left bare,
I find peace of heart

as winter hides itself
beneath the ice and snows,
I find peace of heart

as spring time draws us
into warmth and comfort light,
I find peace of heart

as summer swells and
days run long with laughter bright,
I find peace of heart

Wisdom Speaks

wisdom speaks within
the carved out, cultivated,
quiet hours of day

Earnest Truth

peace runs freely through
the quiet of restful minds,
speaking earnest truth

Let the Warmth of Dawn

let the warmth of dawn
ignite your soul, and 'waken
you to live and love

Hope: a triptych

at times, *it* is a
horizonless sky, wide, open,
blanketing in view

it can also be
a speck of sand, lost to the
folds of hand's tight grip

both are just, as it
takes mountains'n'valleys, both
to build a landscape, full

unlock the safe

un-entraped
by
canvas
winds,
swaying
branches,
both
bare and stale

to live
beyond
one's
past

to have
endured

to have
survived
tasteless
skies

to live
unwrapped
safe
at rest

Look to the Sunrise Bright

Look to the sunrise bright
to overtake the night's clear hold
-- replacing tepid-cold's
icy touch. When the golden rays
Of dawn arrive, the day
will rule -- and he will praise the song
of morning, that which longs
for the gathered throngs of fire.

The Softness Comes as Dawn

The softness comes as dawn once more will turn,
as shadows flee -- will cower in its wake.
The light will rise to watch the darkness burn.

The harshness of one's past is cause to churn
Sad memories their minds find hard to take.
The softness comes as dawn once more will turn,

So place your mind up to the light and spurn
The creeping mists - there's far too much at stake.
The light will rise to watch the darkness burn.

Surround yourself with those who will return
And stand with you amidst the toil at stake.
The softness comes as dawn once more will turn.

In future hopes, we need ourselves discern,
Those dreams within, we must allow to wake.
The light will rise to watch the darkness burn.

The choice is ours to make, it's ours to learn,
Which seeds we grow, which life we choose to make.
The softness comes as dawn once more will turn,
The light will rise to watch the darkness burn.

My Mind, It Will Return to Me

My mind, it will return to me,
If patience I hold true and just,
The cracks may heal and set me free -
My mind, it will return to me,
Then peace would stay, pray never flee,
To build the life I need and must -
My mind, it will return to me,
If patience I hold true and just.

I Find that I am in Love with the Light

I find that I am in love with the night,
Perhaps it is naught but an ache for the sun.
If ever the moon and the stars were done,
I would sprint toward dawn to burn with the bright.

Is it attraction of illumined might
Or captured affections that have me won?
I find that I am in love with the night,
Perhaps it is naught but an ache for the sun.

Both may still or propel me to flight.
Both may inspire - cause passions to run.
Is it mere glittering beams that stun
Or the presence of warmth that feels so right?
I find that I am in love with the light.

AFTERWORD

Imagine Pt. 2

Looking back—
Looking back at foundations,
Which over time had
Crumbled—
Had broken down,
Tumbled to the
ground

They would no longer suit—

A choice—
A choice to rebuild, to reset the
Corner stone...again,
Replace each brick and
Beam,
Each stone.

Imagine what life can
Be if we allow ourselves to
Dream.

AUTHOR'S NOTE

Hold to what hope you've found. Treasure it. Cherish its warmth and glow. This journey of healing continues in the next collection of poetry entitled: *Among the Wildflowers*. Coming Spring of 2023.

Craig Randall, March 2022